Demons in the Cellar:

Reprogram Your Subconscious to Escape
The Shackles of Abuse and Trauma -
Change Your Mind, Change Your Life!

Tim Ebl

Disclaimer

When examining psychological issues and traumatic experiences, professional advice should be obtained. This book is intended for informational purposes only, and the author cannot be held responsible for any use of this book which attempts to replace professional help and guidance from a qualified professional counsellor.

Scary topics such as mental and physical abuse, poverty, alcohol addiction and suicidal thoughts will be discussed. Any individual that will be "triggered" and adversely affected by the candid discussion of these topics, should stop here. The author will not accept responsibility for anything that might occur from reading past this point. Unless we are talking about positive results, then - by all means - blame me! ^_^

Table of Contents

Chapter 1
Haunted

Every day, we make decisions and take actions that deeply affect our outcomes and happiness. We raise our children, talk to our co-workers and run our businesses, thinking that we are in control of our decisions. But most often, we aren't really deciding. We are on autopilot, and the pilot is all of the experiences in our past - good or bad. We don't even see the demons and ghosts that are there constantly; whispering in our ears and getting us to fly the plane of our lives into the blackest clouds full of lightning.

The average person is completely unaware of the beliefs and conditioning that guides their every thought. They glide through life as a sleepwalker, bumping into things and creating messes that they have to deal with during their brief waking periods. Sometimes they sleepwalk right off of a cliff! We see these people, the ones that were forced out of "normal" society, and wonder how they ended up living on the street. It could be their demons got the best of them.

Negative programming and conditioning ruins things. It means we don't reach our potential. Our dreams are dropped in the mud, and trampled upon when life bumps us with events on the path. If we don't find a way to pick those dreams up and wipe the gunk off of them, they are forgotten and left behind. The world is a lesser place for it; the more people who are living their dreams, the better off we all are!

We teach our children limiting beliefs, and crush their hopes. Our actions around our children are their biggest learning tool. We pack them full of the programming we received all of our lives, and then send them on their way with hope. That hope is foolish if we filled them with self-defeating beliefs and demons of our making. No-one wants their sons and daughters to go out and make all the same mistakes we did, but that's quite often exactly what happens. We owe it to our children to give them every fighting chance, and that might mean we need to change the ways we relay negative programming to them. The only way to do this is to remove it from our own minds.

We don't get ahead at work. Our personalized way of looking at reality stops us from interacting with customers and co-workers that will give us the best results. We have conflicts in the workplace. We don't get promotions and raises. We hate our jobs and can't see a way out. All due to our negative programming. Since such a large percentage of our time is spent at work, we really need to make sure that we can at least tolerate our days. Mental routines that make us hate our occupations need to go; we need to feel good about our contribution, and that can improve at any job.

We have less fulfilling friendships, and heartbreaking relationships. Our expectations and hopes are dashed to the rocks again and again, never seeing how the build-up of beliefs and programming are actually the cause of these failures. Romantic beginnings start out with so much promise, but then explode like a failed shuttle launch as the demons come out and sabotage the mission. What if we could find those short circuits and faulty emotional reactions, and remove them forever? We could start living a more authentic life, not just re-enacting learned behavior and past disasters.

We have failed businesses and burnt bridges. We end up depressed and in poor shape physically, emotionally and mentally.

Following the programming of society, we eat too much and exercise too little. When we do try to improve, subroutines of inertia and the deep-seated belief that we really don't deserve to get better stop us in our tracks.

But there is hope. We don't need to let the ghosts and demons from our past run our lives into the dirt of despair. There are tools and techniques that I can show you, resources that are powerful and easy to use. You aren't the problem - your ghosts and demons are. They were given to you by your parents, your environment, society, and the world. I can show you how to free yourself. Pick your dreams back up out of the mud, wipe them off, and chose your own path. See some of those icebergs in the water, and steer the boat around them. Fly your plane toward clear sky and avoid those thunderstorms on the horizon.

I'm an example of what abuse and poverty can do to a child. Limiting beliefs and negativity were crammed into me as a youngster. It caused me to make many tragic decisions and caused a lot of grief for myself as well as for my wife and children. I spent years using alcohol abuse, overworking, video games and relationships with abusers to distract myself from the damage inside me. It eventually came to a head and nearly destroyed everything for me.

All this was due to the programming I got from my childhood and how I reacted to it. I spent years fighting depression. I destroyed us financially more than once. I couldn't make real friendships. I was in deep emotional pain and refused to seek help.

That's all behind me now.

I found ways to examine the demons in my cellar, let them out, and shoo them on their way. I've released limiting beliefs and information that I was trained to use from my earliest memories. I reduced the impact of traumatic, abusive events. I rooted out the poverty thinking that caused me to sabotage our financial lives. I learned techniques that anyone can use to improve their inner lives immeasurably and

I will teach you all about it if you keep reading.

Don't let these issues come to a head and derail you like they nearly did to me. I almost ended my second marriage and was on the verge of sinking into a deep depression with no bottom. I suspect that if I went there, I would never have gotten out, I would have chosen to leave this world. Luckily, I found ways to deprogram myself. You can use them too.

Even if you think you don't have any of these issues, this book can help you. We are all filled with unhelpful programming from television, school, organizations and people. We have damaging beliefs about our weight and body image, about money, and about success. Some of the techniques I will teach you in this book can help in those areas. You will be surprised by the results! What if you could change the way you start out every day, so that you were filled with positive reactions and freedom from negative self-talk? That's what I accomplished for myself, and it didn't take years to accomplish.

My promise to you is this: stick with this book and try the techniques, and you will have a greater understanding of how your life has gone so far. You will feel more peace and happiness. You will attract better results in the future. You will lose those limiting beliefs and get the courage you need to reach for your dreams. You'll have better relationships. You will be free of your past and ready to write your own story. You can start each day ready to take on the world!

You aren't the problem, the Programming and beliefs that you absorbed are!

You owe it to yourself to start this journey now. Don't miss out on the methods that can help you to free yourself from past limitations. Find happiness and reach your goals. Your life partner, children and close friends are counting on you to be the best person you can be. If you don't yet have these people in your life, you can maximize your chances of finding them by ditching your negative programming.

Take action and take control of your own mind. Keep reading to find out how to evict those demons and ghosts and start living.

Chapter 2:
From Almost Happy, to Almost Alive

I was successful. I had three children and a devoted wife. There were a couple of new vehicles in the driveway; I was a supervisor at work, and we owned our own home with no mortgage. We had a lot going for us in the material world. I really believed that we were on the right track; that we were winning at this thing called life. I even managed to lose 25 pounds and seemed to be in good shape all around.

I read self help books and worked on being the best person I could possibly be. I owned more self-help books than anyone I knew, from mindfullness to self-hypnosis. Even though I saw very little progress, I kept on buying books and consuming them like candy. I felt like I was better than others because I was trying to improve; never mind that I usually never followed through on the advice from one book before I ran to the next. A true self-help junkie.

I thought I was optimistic; that I knew what the world was about. But I really had surface happiness. Consciously, I was happy, or at least, I told myself I was.

I was delusional. I had no idea the demons in my cellar were about to emerge and have their say. These were all shallow, material things that I had made my life out of. It was a flimsy sham. All it needed was enough stress to crack the shell. As life would have it, a large hammer showed up to smack me around and dump me out of my cosy delusion.

It was around this time of my arrogant optimism, that I got laid off, with no job prospects on the horizon. Every employer was downsizing, and the economy was in bad shape. It was 2009; everyone was having a hard time. There had been warning signs for over a year, but we ignored them. I should have seen the layoff coming, had I not been soaked in false positives. I was totally unprepared and out of money in a few weeks.

I wasn't too worried at first. But as I began my job search, I was turned down repeatedly. I needed better qualifications to get another job, and I allowed myself to be left behind in the qualifications arms race that is life. I was out of work for eight months and didn't know what to do. I looked for work even harder. Daily I visited the offices of every company in range, dropping off resumes. I didn't get a single call- back. I started looking for jobs farther from home, and I emailed more resumes.

As the money dried up and we were forced to look at our finances, we realized that credit card debt and vehicle loans were totally out of control. Without a job, banks wouldn't help me. We were living on borrowed time - soon to be homeless. We owed more than $20,000 on just one credit card and the total debt was unimaginably high. We asked for loans from family members and got turned down.

All day every day, the phone was ringing. It wasn't job offers or help, it was collection agencies. They were rude and abusive. We couldn't pay our bills, so they kept phoning. It's hard to feel good about your life with those people on the other end of the phone line.

Studies have found links between job loss and heart attacks. I can believe it. Being unemployed and watching your life spiral down the drain, is demeaning... heartbreaking. When you base your life on being a valuable worker, you find yourself useless as an unemployed person. The entire banking and credit system judges you as unfit, unwanted, a complete waste of human life.

Family life started deteriorating. There were many fights between me and my wife, with shouting and nearly-violence on both our parts. Our children had to witness these exchanges of frustration and emotional pain, something I will always regret. I considered leaving, runnning away. My wife asked me if it was over and I couldn't answer her right away. My heart was breaking; I couldn't feel love coming from her, and I couldn't see any way out of this corner we painted ourselves into.

My oldest son broke down crying one day and told me he wished we weren't so poor. It made me really angry - I saw red. How dare he? He had no idea what poor was! I'm still ashamed of the yelling I did that day.

Being told we were poor by one of my children was the breaking point in my mind.

Disillusionment

That day was all the opening that my demons needed to slip their bindings. They were so well hidden that I forgot they even existed. In my strange view of the world, I had a glowing and happy childhood filled with rainbows and unicorns.

Here's some of my forced false positives: I thought I came from a positive upbringing, and only had fond memories of growing up. I thought

I went to the best school in the area, the one that turned out some of the pillars of society. Anything that happened to me in school was just a learning experience that made me a better person.

Growing up poor was good for me. I learned useful life lessons. We did the best with what we had; and the things we didn't have, was a choice my parents made. They were happy living a simple life. People with new cars and big homes weren't as happy as we were; they paid dearly for their comfortable lifestyles.

Anyone who made the big time must have given up so much. We were better off poor. Money can't buy happiness. Camels, needles, rich men and heaven.

This imaginary past of mine was hiding a poverty mentality of the worst kind. It was covering up how unloved I felt, and how much I hated myself. The cloud of positive thinking shielded me from the negative truths of my memories and feelings.

Terrible things existed in my past, but I just didn't think about them. As far as I was concerned, affirmations and mental tricks were all I needed to move on. I knew The Secret, after all. I had the cat in the bag.

Maybe I needed that shield. It could be that I needed to grow as a person before I could face the truth and grow past it. But losing my job, my marriage on the rocks, and maybe losing all of our belongings, released an emotional storm in me. Now, I was the adult that was forcing my children to be poor! The cat was clawing its way out of that bag, looking for vengeance.

I was forced to feel what lived inside of me full on.

It was as though the ignored feelings from my childhood were magnified by suppressing them all of those years. I avoided the pain for so long, and now it was time to turn and face it.

I became completely disillusioned with life. Everything went from black and white, right and wrong, to a uniform grey of meaninglessness. Other than my children, everything seemed pointless. Depression dragged me right back to my

deepest programming, which was developed in my childhood. The demons were loose, and they started making me run through every terrible thing that had ever happened to me.

Chapter 3

Where the Demons Came From

At the risk of giving it all away, I feel that I should warn you. This next section will be hard to read, because my past is a giant train wreck. A trigger warning is in order. The faint of heart should call it quits right about now. Go past this point and accept responsibility for accepting knowledge. If you think that you won't be able to control any reactions it might cause in your own emotions and thoughts, stop here.

Having said that, anyone who is going to need to stop here, should seek professional help. This is the time to work on those parts of yourself. You deserve to go through life as whole as you can. Don't accept your limitations; there can always be improvement and growth. I know that for me, it wasn't enough to just accept victim status and live with it. I needed to move past that.

I'm going to show you the experiences that gave me such negative programming, so that you can recognize that there are ways to change your thinking. I'm not writing this to make you feel sorry for me or to blame anyone. These events just exist in memory form now. They are what they are. I accept them, and focus on moving on. I'm not the same person who lived through these events, and neither are the adults who were in my life. In any case, they were victims of their own demons and ghosts. The chain of causality goes back deep into the past. If mental programming and enforced beliefs and thinking can cause our actions, then can they truly take full blame for their harmful actions?

Later in the book, I will share with you my secret technique for dealing with dramatic events. When you gain power over these events, they can no longer make you feel bad. In order for you to see that the techniques really did work for me, I need you to understand just how bad my memories were. It wasn't surface level damage; it was deep and pervasive thoughts and feelings that I needed to change. It affected every part of my life: what jobs I applied for, what kind of friends I had, how I raised my children, even what food I ate.

At the same time, many people have suffered through much more than me. Daily, people endure abuse, suffering, and PTSD that make my problems seem small and unimportant. I feel that the techniques I have learned could be useful for these people too.

Everything is relative. I don't mean to compare my life with anyone else's life. Since we are all individuals, what affected me in one way, wouldn't necessarily have the same impact on you or someone else. Everyone has their story. I just know mine the best and I know how I felt while I was in the thick of it.

Here goes. Bear with the story, I promise the outcomes will be worth it!

From the beginning, I was shown how hard and painful life was.

I grew up thinking that we were poor, because we didn't deserve more. I knew that life wasn't fair; that we couldn't get what we wanted, and that we didn't deserve what all of our neighbours had.

All we had was an old house built in the 40's, with a plain plank floor and a dirt cellar. Basements were for rich people. There was a trap door in the floor in the middle of the kitchen, and a ladder down to where we kept the root vegetables. I was afraid of what was down there; mice, spiders, monsters even.

We had single pane windows and no insulation, in a place where winter temperatures reached lows of -45 Celsius in the winter. Our only heat source was the wood stove that we cooked on, or a dog you could snuggle up to. I had a couple old woolen army blankets and no sheets on my bed. We never used sheets, never washed our bedding.

I had to sleep with my clothes on in the winter to keep from freezing. I didn't have pajamas.

We weren't surrounded by poverty. All of the other kids at school had plenty of food and newish clothing. At least hand-me downs from the same era. I was wearing bell bottom cords from the sixties and seventies. That's all I had. Imagine going through grades one to four wearing only clothes that someone else threw away. There was a lot of teasing and bullying over just this one issue.

We were also the only family I knew that didn't have running water. I went to school dirty and probably smelly, every single day. No washing machine, I washed my own clothes in a basin once a week because I was so embarrassed. I only had a few changes of clothes. I felt dirty and disgusting. I did the best I could. We went to a laundromat once a month, whether we needed it more frequently, or not.

There was no cleaning done in our house. If you've ever watched the show

Hoarders, then you've seen the home I grew up in. There were piles of garbage covering up the couch, and the kitchen table would go weeks without being seen. Bags of leftover stuff and dirty clothes rotted quietly by themselves under newspapers and fliers.

There's a difference between poor, and slovenly. These kinds of conditions create a special kind of shame when you grow up in it. You can't invite other kids to your house, because they will see how you live. You can't talk about it to adults, because they will look at you with pity. You have to pretend everything is wonderful - just a big happy party - at your house. I learned to fake happiness, to put on a good front.

Before I came into the picture, my parents were like many other young couples. They worked and they loved each other. They had adventures out hiking and exploring. They had dreams and they were optimistic. Between the two of them they even managed to afford a piece of property and a new truck. It was a green '66 Chevy with three in the tree.

I can imagine Dad being just like everyone else: going to work and being productive. My father was a welder, and he worked at a large, reputable company. I know this was a good time for them. I've heard the stories.

So, what made him retreat from the world and drive us into poverty? The voices in his head.

He wasn't insane. He was programmed. His father - my grandfather - laid the groundwork for depression and self-hate. My dad was optimistic and had big plans, but then, he chose to listen to the wrong voices in his head.

Have you ever heard the Cherokee story about the two wolves living inside of each person? The wolves are fighting to the death. One wolf feeds on negatives like anger, shame and fear. The other wolf feeds on joy, peace and generosity. Which wolf will win? The one you feed the most.

My dad decided to feed the bad wolf, every day of his life. At first he fed both wolves, but slowly, the negatives outweighed the positives. The evil wolf backed the good wolf into a corner and snarled at the world. His family had to pay for his decisions.

Maybe my mom had no choice. It's nice to think that she was a product of the times, and that she didn't have many options.

It's also true that she made the choice to stay. She made the choice to accept her fate. It was easier than doing something about it. I guess she had her own programming and demons.

That new truck didn't get washed for years. We drove around in it dirty. Driving down back roads, you couldn't tell it was green anymore; it was just a big pile of rusty mud.

At some point, I decided it needed to be washed. I'm not sure how old I was, but old enough to see that everyone else was capable of washing their vehicles. No one asked me to do it. I hand pumped a bucket of water and found a couple old shirts for rags which I used to hand wash that truck. I did it because I was so ashamed to be seen in town in such a dirty truck. I was terrified that someone we knew would see how we lived.

He never changed the oil, nor did any maintenance and the motor quit working eventually. You can't drive 50,000 miles without changing the oil and expect good things to happen. That was the last new vehicle my father bought

Abuse, Misuse and Secrets

I don't know the true extent of the sexual dysfunction and abuse in my family, but I do know that I got off lightly. There were people who were treated even worse than me. I didn't know about the others until much later. I grew up thinking I was the only one. I won't mention the others specifically, because that's not my story to tell. I'm also not going to go over every event that occurred to me, because there were several and with different perpetrators. I am however going to discuss the one instance that left the most visible memories and effects.

I was sexually abused as a very young boy by my teenaged male cousin, who used to visit the farm and help out with chores. He was always friendly to me, and no one would have suspected what he did. He came across as the nicest guy, definitely everyone's pal.

I was sitting on the floor one day, wearing only my underwear and a shirt, playing with my astronaut toy. It was a white plastic figurine of a man in a space suit, scooping up moon rocks with a weird, long-handled scoop. I wasn't aware of being eyed up like a sex object. The way he looked at me, I can see now there was lust involved. It was shortly after this day that he managed to get me alone the first time.

Why would someone sexually abuse a defenceless child? What kind of twisted and evil sicko would do such a thing? The answer isn't simple. I don't think abusers are evil. I think they were programmed to do it. Maybe it was done to them, or maybe they witnessed abuse. The idea had to come from somewhere.

I do think that they are responsible for their actions; they made choices that resulted in hurting someone else. The effects on that kid last a lifetime. It can't be undone. It's a lot like when Luke Skywalker's hand was lopped off by his father. He can get a prosthetic robot hand, but it will never be the same.

I got a prosthetic robot set of feelings and reactions. I faked my way through being normal, but I was never the same. And I was terrible at faking normal.

I will never know why my cousin decided he needed to have sex with me when I was five. He might have thought I wouldn't remember it when

I got older, that it didn't cause any real harm. If that was his thinking, he was very wrong.

I have very vivid memories of my childhood. Maybe it would have been better if I didn't. I remember quite clearly the day my baby brother came home from the hospital when I was three. I remember my mom breastfeeding him. I remember sitting the hospital parking lot in that dirty green '66 Chevy truck changing the settings on the radio and heater, all alone, because my dad left a three-year old in the parking lot.

So, I remember what was done to me. I'm quite certain that bad things happened, and that I didn't cause it in any way. All the sights and sounds of an 18-year old "loving" a five-year old. I think the smells are the worst; I still avoid certain things because of it. I remember the dirty aftermath, being cleaned up so no one would know. "Don't tell anyone about this! They'll be mad at you," he told me every time it was over. I was afraid that I would be in trouble. My dad could never find out.

Now, here's the dilemma I was left with: Before this, I really liked my cousin. He would come over and spend hours playing games with me. He was my hero. I didn't have anyone else around, except my little brother, and that meant I wanted to be everywhere my cousin went. And then, I was betrayed. Something happened between us that I didn't really understand. I knew no one was ever supposed to find out, a secret. And, everyone loved him. My mom worshipped the ground her nephew walked on. The whole family loved him. He was their best and brightest. The rapist. He may have done this to others in the family; in fact why wouldn't he?

After a while, I did try to talk to my mom about this. She refused to believe me. It was an open and shut thing, it never happened and I had better never speak lies like that again. I was really upset, but I buried it.

Later on, when I started becoming interested in girls, I would remember what happened. I wondered, am I gay? I would know, right? I was afraid of any girl/boy contact. Not that I had a lot of opportunities, with how the other kids saw me. I was always on the outside, never part of the group. It was as much the way I acted as how they treated me, but I was trapped in my own misery.

Acting Out

By the time I was six, I wasn't the same kid. I remember BTR (before the rape) being happy, playing, friendly. I remember laughing out loud. I was ashamed of that happy, playful kid. He felt so cocky and naive, and trusting.

I remember ATR that I was a liar who stole anything I could get my hands on. Lying was my business, and business was good. I was incapable of owning up to anything, it was always someone else's fault.

I swiped gum and candy from the local store. I was caught and humiliated. I stole toys from other children and got beat up for it. I took any tool of my father's that wasn't strapped down and hid it in the bushes, quite often forgetting where. If I was lucky enough to find money, I stole that too. I blamed everything I did on my little brother, and sometimes he got a beating instead of me. That was the worst; I was ashamed of causing him so much suffering. But I did it again.

I took my dad's rolling papers and tobacco and tried to smoke. I never quite got the hang of it - at least not until I was a teenager.

After watching my dad siphon gas one day, I learned how to do that too. My first try at sucking the siphon hose ended with me accidentally swallowing some gas. A little more practice, and there was no stopping me. I stole gas out of vehicles and lit fires with the matches I took. Luck was on my side in that I never burnt any buildings down by accident. When we were caught, I played dumb, or blamed my brother.

My father reacted to all of this with anger. In a sense, I understand that he felt he was completely out of control of this situation. He believed in the saying *spare the rod and spoil the child* . He also lost complete control of himself whenever I misbehaved, which was anytime I was awake. I was on the receiving end of brutal beatings, all of which I remember and have had to deal with as an adult.

There was never an improvement in my behaviour after all of the spankings, whippings and raging that I was subjected to. As soon as the pain wore off, I was back to lying and stealing. I just got better at it, so I wouldn't get caught. One thing that didn't change for years, was being blamed for everything that went missing.

Dad made sure we knew how we were wrecking his life. He told us we were stupid. He muttered how we were monkeying around with everything. My brother and I were totally ignored, except when it was time for us to be punished - verbally or physically. There wasn't a positive male role model in the house. I was never touched by my father for comfort or play, only in anger.

And he was right; I did steal from him and lie to him. I was a troublemaker, day in and day out. I didn't know why, I just did it. I was any parent's worst nightmare, uncontrollable and untameable.

I Was Filled with Fear

Fear gets into every part of your life. Fear of being hit. Fear of being yelled at. Fear of going to school and being laughed at. Fear of having strangers look at you funny because your clothes are ragged and dirty.

Fear of not getting enough food and never having what everyone else gets to eat.

Fear of my parents, my "protectors."

Fear of sex.

And it all boils down to one basic fear for me: Being afraid that I was unlovable, that there was something wrong with me. Afraid of the ultimate rejection, that I was alone and worthless.

My father had anger issues. There was a lot of yelling. Dad liked to throw his tantrums. I recall all of our dishes, pots and pans being thrown out on the cold, snowy front yard one Christmas Eve, and many other items being launched across the house in a violent rage. I remember being taken out to the car to sit in the back seat while my mom huddled behind the wheel and cried, and not knowing what to do.

I was in training. I was learning to turn into the Hulk to force people to give in to fear. I found out that one way to not be afraid was to get angry.

There's one specific memory which sums up the relationship I had with my father, and fear. He was running a chainsaw, cutting up some firewood. Listening to the roar of the saw engine, and watching the sawdust fly. The blade cut through wood so easy!

I decided that he might just turn with the saw and cut me up like a bloody tree. It would be so easy for him to finish me off, once and for all.

Problem solved. No more stupid, troublemaking kid hanging around, making his life harder. In fact, why wouldn't he want to. He must have thought of it already.

I kept backing away until I thought I was safe. Then, I got yelled at because I wasn't helping move the blocks of wood. Trapped. Forced to approach and help stack wood while someone I couldn't trust used an incredibly dangerous, brutal tool right behind me.

I was terrified of my father, and forced to spend a lot of time watching him to make sure I could stay safe. Death seemed like a strong possibility; I knew it was only a matter of time. Fear was a constant undercurrent. But I knew I was a bad kid, so I deserved whatever was coming.

Keep It In The Family

We had a lot of huge family gatherings. They took place on every holiday. At least once a month, everyone gathered at my grandma and granddad's house. We had group birthday parties, for everyone whose birthdays were close together. On the surface, these seemed like loving family gatherings.

I now wonder how many people in the room were just really good at pretending to be happy, like me. Maybe they all were really good at hiding their demons. In fact, I'm now absolutely sure that several of my relatives suffered worse than I did.

These parties weren't all bad; I did have some good times there. I always knew we were going to get better food than at home, and I would play with relatives my age. My grandparents seemed so happy to host these gatherings.

There was an insidious undercurrent to these gatherings for me. My cousin would be there, or his mother would be there, talking about what he was up to. He was a constant presence in my life. When he was around, I would be afraid to look him in the eye to see if he was thinking about it; if there was any guilt or fear there. I was scared that the truth would come out and everyone would hate me for ruining him, somehow. My mom and my aunts loved him so much; they just tolerated me because they had to. I faked my way past all of these encounters.

He would talk to me like nothing happened. He acted like a friend. I didn't do a thing about it, and I felt betrayed by myself. I pretended I liked him, and talked to him in front of others.

After I got older, I dreamed of outing him, revealing the rapist in their midst. He moved away and became a nurse, and I lost my chance.

Especially with my constant bad behaviour, I doubt anyone was ever happy to see me. Not to mention how my brother and I were perpetually dirty and half starved; it must have been like letting animals in the house. I knew this about us, too. I hated everything about our lives; I was so ashamed of my parents and of me. I think that I was rude, and abrupt, and shy. I couldn't be any other way.

Every Night Was Torture

I was an insomniac as a little boy.

I laid awake at night reliving bad things that happened to me. While everyone else in the house slept, I remembered the bad things I did. Running through the experiences over and over, I felt ashamed of getting caught stealing or lying. It was common to go over an incident of shame and feel absolutely horrible, wanting to die.

I went through the times I was abused; I remembered every embarrassing thing from school. I lived the bullying and teasing again every night.

I didn't know it at the time, but I was pulling all of the worst bits of my life together into a big ball of terrible. I was reinforcing the bad, never seeing any good. I was doing the opposite of meditation.

There were a lot of nightmares. Sleep wasn't fun. I woke up scared so many times, that I became afraid of the night. I didn't dare call out after everyone was sleeping, as there would be hell to pay if I woke Dad up in the middle of the night. That was like waking up an angry bear. More fear.

From Acting Out, to Depressed Teenager

More time passed and I turned into a withdrawn, depressed teenager. I made "friends" with a red-head boy, who picked on me and put me down every day of my life. He pushed me around, called me names, and mercilessly tortured me. But he was willing to let me hang around. When you don't have any friends, you aren't very picky. He was cruel and I liked it. I let him put me down and laugh at me, and I always came back for more.

I spent hours thinking about suicide. Sitting and wallowing in my bad feelings like a pig in mud. I was totally bogged down and stuck. It's a good thing there were no examples of it, no other teen suicides in my area, or I would have probably done it. I really didn't see any point in my miserable life. I was a complete loser and I knew it.

Since I couldn't bring myself to end it, I committed emotional suicide instead. As soon as I had access to alcohol through bootleggers and older teens, I started stealing money to get booze. I took binge drinking to a whole new level. I drank at every available opportunity. A lot. I could be found puking my guts out in a ditch, in a bathroom, or in some bushes. If I had lived in a place with hard drugs, you wouldn't be reading this story right now, because I would've ended up dead. I lived to party. I was almost one of the cool kids at this part of my life; finally finding something in common with my classmates, who were at parties and dances.

I never considered any further education after high school. While everyone else was busy making plans, I was sure that that was not for me. I literally thought that was for the rich kids. And to me, everyone else was the rich kids. I was the dirty, outcast, poor kid that wasn't good enough for any of that.

I had an 87% average. I tried really hard in school, because I wanted to impress my parents. I'm not sure why, looking back now. Another sad reality was that, no matter how good my report card was - no-one seemed to care. There's no impressing people who won't pay attention to you. I was on the honour roll. I could have gotten a scholarship, a grant, a student loan, but I never even considered this as an option. No authority figures bothered to step up and suggest anything to me. I really still can't believe nobody cared or paid any notice to me, but while teachers were busy helping the other students prepare for college and university I just quietly shrank into the background.

If you're a teacher, a parent, or any adult that cares, don't let this happen to a child in your care.

It's a crime to let people waste their talents when you have the power to help them achieve their potential. If you see that kid who doesn't have a plan, talk to him or her. Maybe it's because they're depressed, have low self esteem, or are almost suicidal. Maybe they need a friend.

Find out if they have dreams. If they don't, suggest a few dreams. I really wish someone would have stepped up and done ANYTHING. Who knows what kind of difference that could have made?

Free From School, Trapped By My Programming

What kind of existence is in store for a teenager who gets out of school with zero plans, few friends and no support system? It's a miracle I didn't get into worse trouble. I did what I had to do to survive, but it wasn't pretty: dishwasher at a cafe, farm worker, several different hard labour jobs. It sounds ridiculous, but I actually somehow ended up digging a ditch by hand for one week that first summer out of my parent's house. It really happened. I was a ditch digger.

I had no idea that I could do more. I didn't even think of getting an apprenticeship for a trade. My low self esteem and thoughts of poverty led me to hang out with people at the bottom of the social ranks. I didn't talk to people who had secondary education of any kind. Those kinds of people were literally on a different playing field from me. I belonged with the dregs of society. I was one level above homeless; barely getting by, and I thought that my lot in life was to clean, dig and carry for others.

How did I end up in this mess?

A couple years of this and I managed to get a coveted spot working on an oil rig. A glorified labourer. The work was hard and the environment was rough. Workers were motivated by the constant screaming and belittling of their superiors. If you were late for work, even once, you were fired. Days were 12 hrs long, with 14-

day shifts. I spent hours doing work covered in oil and mud, with the driller yelling at me, and the other men playing stupid pranks on me. I found the perfect job; it was where I belonged.

An Abusive Relationship

I found a girl who seemed to be the one. We fell in love and got married. It wasn't all bad, because without her, I never would have gained my amazing first son. I wouldn't trade him in for anything.

That marriage, on the other hand...

A lot of people don't believe that women can be the abusers. I don't know what rock they live under. I was mentally and emotionally abused for the year that we managed to stay together after the wedding. She was my next bully, and calling me names was just the beginning.

Things started to escalate into violence. She punched me in the face hard enough to loosen teeth. She threw butcher knives at me. If that girl hadn't been such a lousy knife thrower, I would have been a goner. If you've never had a large knife thrown at you, then you aren't living. Or at least, you aren't living in absolute fear that your significant other might actually kill you.

Once, there was an argument about who got to use the car. I needed to take my infant son across town. She needed to go hang out with a friend. I lost the argument, put my son in the stroller, and started walking.

Half way there, a car pulled up to the curb. My car. She leaned out of the car and threw something at me, hitting me. As it fell on the sidewalk I realized it was the watch I gave her earlier that spring.

She drove off as I stood there, speechless. I pushed the stroller for a couple more miles.

She needed to get out and party. I needed to work my twelve hour day and then get up in the middle of the night to warm up a bottle in the microwave, feed my son, and put him back to bed. There was no balance. And I did it all; I let myself get used right up. I would have done anything for her. I knew that love was pain. She was causing me pain, because I was in love.

I thought I deserved this. It was the way it was supposed to be. My programming was a rock solid barrier to anything good happening in my life. Relationships weren't about happiness; they were about subjugation, and I ended up on the bottom.

It all ended when she started sleeping around. My first wife ended up getting pregnant from the pizza guy, on our balcony. My ex neighbour told me the story, because he saw them out there.

We broke up. I still might have stayed with her, if she hadn't left me. After everything she put me through, I still begged her to stay. She was going to leave me, and instead of letting her walk out I actually abandoned all of my belongings by moving out instead. I sacrificed everything I owned for her, except a small bag of clothes and a ten speed bike.

I never gave up on my son, and spent years putting up with her abuse so I could take him for visits. I did everything I could to be there for him.

A while later, I found the love of my life and got married again. I settled into being nearly happy, and I forced all of those skeletons firmly into their closets, while throwing a rug over the cellar door to keep the ghouls down there. I got custody of my first son and we started building a life together. Two more children arrived. We moved up in the world.

I thought I beat the past, but I was wrong.

There's no question, I had accumulated a lot of baggage. But I was a survivor. Despite years of depression, destructive behaviour, and dumb choices, I was still alive and kicking. I tried hard to do what I thought I was supposed to do.

One major concern I had, was making sure my father got to have grandchildren. I still don't understand the mixed up thinking and beliefs that could convince me I had to do things to make my father happy, after all of the suffering he caused me. Still, I wanted to do things to keep my parents happy, and I was ready to sacrifice my life to make it happen.

I truly believed that things were good with my upbringing. I was making the best of things. I was trying to squeeze those lemons and make a nice batch of lemonade.

If you want to make a fancy shirt, but all you have is a garbage bag and some scotch tape, what are you going to end up with? At best, a really crappy poncho. At worst, a broken garbage bag. You can't make a shirt out of that.

The same goes for happiness and a positive spirit. No matter what you do with garbage, it's lower quality.

Read on to find out how I sabotaged everything good that I was building in my life, and how I finally found the secrets that set me free.

Chapter 4
Programmed

Years passed, and I seemed to be making it. I forgot all about the bad stuff. I thought I was a positive person, and on the surface I seemed to have trained myself to be a positive thinker. This was just an illusion; I had bought into the idea that positive thinking can make big changes easily. I read quite a few personal growth books over the years, and did my best to follow their instructions. But when you are programmed on a deep, subconscious level to know that you're worthless and deserve to be poor, no simple positive thinking affirmations are really going get to the bottom of things.

I used affirmations a lot during the early years of my current marriage. I have notebooks full of written affirmations, which I used to try drive positive thoughts into my mind. I never really got any huge results. I thought I was just doing something wrong, and kept trying. I see now that my demon programming was stronger than my efforts - too hard to root out. It always convinced me that I was wasting my time, that I was lying to myself. I knew deep down that I really didn't love myself, no matter how many times I wrote that I did.

I knew I didn't deserve to have money and more possessions. I knew that I didn't deserve to be happy.

Everyone assumes that optimism and positive thinking are a force for good. This isn't always true. Without a realistic look at what I was doing to myself, my optimistic outlook was like a blanket over a bag of shit. Everything looks neat and tidy, but something still stinks around here. Being optimistic can be a good thing, but not if you let it lull you into inaction, when you need to change.

If a shark bit one arm off of you, and all you thought was "thank God I will still be able to walk," this is optimism. But you'll never walk again, if you bleed to death before you make it to shore. The optimistic thinking about walking was blinding me to the truth that I was bleeding to death.

If you crash land on an island with thirty other people, and you optimistically decide to celebrate being alive by eating the last few tiny packages of snacks, things might turn out ok. Or you might have to turn to cannibalism two months later when no one shows up to rescue you.

If you get married to an abuser, and after some difficult times you manage to escape, you could be optimistic and declare that at least you lived through the experience. You could use your positive thinking to get into another relationship. Your optimism blinds you to the way you attract users and abusers, and how you really have built-in self hate. Instead of doing the things you need to do to set yourself free, the optimism blinds you and you end up being abused, maybe defeated completely.

If you run into money troubles, only to bail yourself out with a consolidation loan, you could use positive thinking and optimism. "This time it'll be different. I got this. We are on top again. Only a few more years added to my debt." And then, your mental programming continues to do what it always did. You fritter away your opportunities like a hungry teenager attacking a bag of potato chips.

Fortunately, you're still optimistic about your chances, though. Even as you have to remortgage your house for the third time. Even as they are closing in to repossess your car.

This happens in casinos every day. Optimism will tell you the next spin will be the win. There's no way you can lose again next time. It will be ok , the optimistic hope tells you. You'll get your mortgage money back; the ball will fall into the right slot the next time for sure. Your thoughts will lead you right to gambling disaster.

I don't see this as optimism or positive thinking, at all. I see it as delusion. And delusion is exactly what books like The Secret and many others might lead you into, if you don't first get those demon thoughts and programming out of your cellar. I'm not saying those books don't and can't help you. I'm suggesting why they don't work for so many people.

Positive thinking is a good concept, but difficult to pull off. "What if I only think positive thoughts? I'll just control everything I think. I can quit thinking negative thoughts if I want to." As if it were so simple! The one big reason this won't work is what we've already seen in these pages. We are all programmed for negativity. The experiences and knowledge we have rammed down our throats has contaminated our minds right to the bottom. Good intentions alone won't change the fact that we haven't been controlling our thoughts, but they've been controlling us.

But what exactly was I doing that was so harmful? What behaviours were giving me such bad results and leading me astray? Stay tuned and we will examine the thinking and beliefs that I was using to approach life. Let's see if you recognize any of these in your own repertoire of behaviors.

Chapter 5

Let's Make Soup

Under my mask of optimism and happiness, I was hiding some truly judgemental and angry core beliefs. I didn't realize what was actually going on inside. I really believed my own smokescreen. That's the power of belief.

If you are familiar with the TV show Seinfeld, you might remember an episode about the Soup Nazi. This character made the best soup; he was a true soup artist. People came from all over to stand in long line-ups, just to get a takeout container of this fabulous soup.

The catch to this fabulous soup was that, if you annoyed the soup Nazi, he would permanently banish you from his establishment. No soup for you! The ultimate in denial of worthiness. There was a strict list of acceptable behaviours at the soup counter. Break the rules and get banished. No soup for you!

Why do I mention this character? Because he embodies many of the behaviours that we find in ourselves. Behaviours which end up banishing us instead of the other way around. The Soup Nazi never questioned his actions. He just reacted with prejudice and no thought.

This also epitomizes the way I ran my life.

Have you ever been minding your own business - maybe at work or at home - and someone mentions how angry you look, completely taking you by surprise? I wonder if this isn't the real meaning of "resting bitchface". Only you will be able to determine if you harbour secret anger, but if you do, it's in your best interest to defuse it.

Other person: "Get up on the wrong side of the bed or something?" Me - startled: "What do you mean?"
Other person: "You look ready to stab someone. Why so angry?" Me - surprised: "I'm not angry!"

This happened to me on many occasions. Apparently, I had "resting bitch face". I always denied being angry. Being told I was angry, made me mad! And on the surface, I felt happy, maybe even positive. I couldn't see or feel any problem. It was like an iceberg spotted in the cold ocean water. That perceptive individual could see the tip of the huge ice mountain; a gigantic block of frozen anger floating beneath the surface. They - of course - stayed clear, sensing the danger. If it got exposed, it could take me over completely.

My favourite anger manifestation was road rage. There's something so liberating about encasing yourself in a couple tons of metal, glass and plastic and entering the road arena to do battle. Just like the classic game Twisted Metal, your clown car of death is out to even the score. Someone cuts you off in traffic. They are blocking YOUR lane! You need to teach the MF'er a lesson! How dare they encroach on your divine right to drive like it's YOUR freeway? No soup for them!

Everyone seems to think they're the best driver on the road. All the rest are driving noobs, clueless and deserving of death by lane change. This is a very common attitude, a deep belief that comes out at the worst of times: when you hold the lives of several other people at hostage. Like your passengers, maybe your children. Innocent drivers that just happen upon your clown car of death. Pedestrians you might not be targeting, but are near the roadside.

A lot of this angry programming that I inherited from my father was about intimidation and control. He would go into a rage and throw things. Then he would swear, threaten, and storm around. My mom would retreat, hide, and cry. I would try to be invisible.

I hated this stuff. It was so hurtful and damaging. Yet, that didn't stop me from acting out the same way when I was triggered. It didn't happen very often, but it was buried in my mind, waiting to come out.

The best triggers were arguments with someone I was in love with. There were some real doozies with my first wife, like Clash of The Titans. Neighbours were scared for their children. Cats and dogs in the vicinity fled for safety. Furniture and walls were broken.

The programming would take over and wreck everything. After it passed, I would feel so terrible. I felt just like my dad. After putting holes in one bedroom wall with my fist, I purposely left the damage as a reminder to myself. I thought it would help me avoid angry, violent outbursts. I only felt shame and guilt when I noticed it each day. I'm not proud of these outbursts. It doesn't matter that I was acting out what I absorbed from a young age. I take full responsibility for the hurts I caused.

I was nothing like my dad. I didn't hit my wife. I had a job; I spent my time trying to improve life for my family. I wanted to be a better person. And I was slowly accumulating the clues that would lead me to defeating this particular demon.

Another trigger for me, was children who didn't obey. When you have this kind of anger demon in you, you can go into a rage whenever the rules get flaunted. I would take it as a personal affront when certain things came up. The absolute worst triggers were one of my boys stealing or lying. So what was the real issue here? What was making me see red?

My children were bringing it all back. That deep part of me remembered exactly what it felt like to be that unhappy little boy. I was dirty, sometimes hungry, and always ashamed. And I lied and I stole things.

Now, my boys were unknowingly reminding me that the little boy inside me was still there. It wasn't conscious at all. I reacted with anger, mostly with yelling and confrontations. Have you ever yelled at your kid, and suddenly realized you just completely demolished them emotionally? Their face scrunched up with bad feelings, tears and snot? These were the parenting skills I was taught. It took a lot to own up to the fact that I was to blame for making someone feel like that.

Again, I was nothing like my father. I didn't insult my children all day every day. I didn't tell them how stupid they were, and I made sure they had clothes that wouldn't make them laughingstocks at school. I read their report cards and tried to encourage them with their dreams. Along with my wife, we did our best to raise them as responsible and loving children.

But I could have done better. I could have cracked the code on the anger demon sooner.

Eventually, I was forced to admit how angry I was with my parents. It was a deep, burning resentment. I was angry with my father the most, but I blamed my mother for not doing anything about it. She accepted the abuse; she let my father abuse us, and she never did a thing.

I was also really angry with the male cousin who raped me. I knew that I would never be able to confront him now, since he passed away and was able to hide from me forever. He did something to me that left deep scars, and never showed any remorse. He always pretended it never happened. Like a coward, I let him get away with it. I went along with the lie; I was there at family events where everyone loved him. I was filled with bitter resentment that he never got his own.

How did I purge the anger? What did I do that finally gave me peace of mind after years of inner turmoil? We're almost there, keep going!

Chapter 6
Ah, My Old Enemy; Ultimatums

When I was small, the most powerful adult in my life used anger as a tool to get what he wanted. Later, I did the same thing. Anger manifests itself in several ways. One way many people use to force results, is the ultimatum. Using these all-or-nothing demands always results in losing trust and damaging relationships, even if the anger is hidden and you seem completely justified in your feelings.

Ultimatums seem like such a good idea at first glance.

"I've got them over a barrel; they would be fools to ignore my demands!" "If you don't stop treating me like this, I'm going to do _____"

"I will leave and deny you everything unless you do _____."

In a selfish world view, the strongest and fastest deserve to win at any cost. However, this is just mental and emotional violence against another person. Their feelings and needs are completely overridden by a one-sided viewpoint and attack.

Don't get me wrong. There are times to place limits and barriers on how you need to be treated. You can decide what your boundaries are, and enforce them as you see fit. Setting boundaries is healthy and a great step forward. This is different from an ultimatum form of attack.

You might be in a situation at work where you need to set limits. "If I am going to be working overtime every weekend, I will ask them to find a way to put me back on my regular schedule or I'll have to find a new job. I'm missing out on too much with the children." This is completely understandable, and a healthy approach to taking care of your needs.

Telling your boyfriend that you won't accept rude treatment from him, is also not what I'm talking about here. That can be a necessary boundary that you need to use for your own good.

The harmful ultimatums I'm thinking of are negatively motivated, where the entire viewpoint is twisted into a selfish direction. There's no give, just take.

It's learned behaviour. People see others doing it and they seem to get results faster than they would if they were "being nice". And maybe they learned it when they were really young, like I did. These behaviours are contagious, like any disease, and they spread.

My pre-loaded software tended to have me mulling over all the perceived bad things that were being done to me. "Still only making __ an hour. I can't believe this. After all of my hard work. They need me. I'm going to force them to pay me more! I am totally unappreciated around here." By amping up the hurt and the anger with more and more sour thoughts, you put yourself in a knot of resentment.

Can you imagine this kind of anger, jealousy, even rage, transmuting into good outcomes? It usually doesn't.

A "do it or else!" attitude is a threat - plain and simple. Bringing this into a relationship proves you're a dangerous unknown. Sometimes you can win temporary concessions this way, but they come with resentment and fear. "You'll be sorry if you don't do this. If I can't force you to do this my way, I'm leaving!" Imagine a loved one doing this to you, how does that make you feel inside?

When a poker player goes on tilt and starts pushing all of his chips in, it's quite often a sign that he stopped thinking rationally and is about to make some really dumb decisions, based completely on emotion. Other players might fear the all in, or they might look for signs of weakness... Ultimatums are like going all in. You give up all control - you're on tilt.

Giving ultimatums at work only ends well for you by accident.

This isn't a strategy, it's a tantrum.

Some parents let their children get away with tantrums, and other parents make them stand in the corner. Either way, acting like an out of control child is a big problem. You could maybe initially "win" in a work situation with a raise or getting your other demands met. In the long run, the relationship with those around you will be changed. It usually doesn't seem to take long before the ultimatum maker moves on, and it's always everyone else' fault that it didn't work out.

Looking back on the times that I tried to manipulate people with a tantrum, I'm not proud. I don't do this anymore. Not only have I learned my lesson the hard way, but I removed the triggers the prompted me to pull this childish trick. I hope you will learn to do the same.

Never Burn a Bridge You Might Need To Use Later

Bridge burners. Not to be confused with the legendary infantry unit from the Malayan Book of The Fallen series by Steven Erikson. Those Bridge burners were damaged soldiers who struggled on against impossible odds. They supported their friends through gruelling battles on several continents; they were legends.

The bridge burners I'm thinking of are cowards who use hit and run, smash and grab tactics. They are legends in their own minds, but their actions leave a trail of emotional destruction and broken relationships.

This used to be me. I'm thankful every day that I'm free of the programming that used to make me think this way.

It's very close to the ultimatum in nature. Take offence or hurt from someone's actions, or even just take offence at their very personality. Then, let these feelings fester and spread like cancer. Quite often the bridge burner will act like nothing is wrong, pretending all is well. Smile and bear it, while twisting up inside like a coiled snake, ready to strike when the time is right.

Bridge burning is all about leaving, burning the bridge down with malice, and walking away feeling smug and superior. A true hit and run, which allows the perpetrator to surprise attack and go free. When executed properly, it stuns the victims speechless.

It happens all the time on social media. After stewing about the terrible things someone has done, the bridge burner crafts a cunning trap. A post is created to leave online, where the unsuspecting victim will find it. It might be public. The post might be humiliating, but will definitely be hurtful. Imagine opening Facebook and finding out that one of your trusted friends said terrible, hurtful things about you. Everyone can see them. Shame and anger fill your heart.

Then the bridge burner unfriends you or blocks you, and you've just been left with no recourse. You can't defend yourself, or ask them why. They win. This kind of scenario has caused suicidal thoughts; it's so damaging and overwhelming.

Bridge burners also like to rage quit jobs. They will let pressures build, and cumulatively the hurtful thoughts stack up to the ceiling of their mind. Finally, they go on tilt. Everyone gets a piece of them, everyone gets what they deserve. And now the bridge burner walks out the door, free of their B.S.

What causes this kind of action? First, the belief that mental violence is a useful skill. Second, role models, which showed the bridge burner how it's done. There's no lack of wonderful bridge burner role models, from parents and relatives, to television and movies, to terrorists attacking the free world. But no matter where the idea comes from, it's the thoughts that we allow ourselves to cherish which can fan the flames and burn the bridge.

Bridge burning gets completely out of control. This thinking leads to terrible things. School shootings and terrorist attacks are the ultimate form. It's an insidious thing, that subconscious programming can lead to murder. I believe that this basic thought pattern is responsible for all of the most violent and terrible atrocities.

I was a bridge burner, and every time it happened I felt justified in my hit and run. Maybe I was wronged, maybe things were unfair. It doesn't matter; I took the coward's way out these situations. It was mostly work situations, and they weren't ideal jobs by any definition. Some of my bosses were outright manipulators. One of them admitted to using guilt and shame against the employees. He had me worked up and angry for months. When I left his employ, I threw a tantrum of epic proportions. I walked out of there free, in the physical sense. In my mind, I was in chains. I was in the black iron prison of my anger and beliefs. Thanks, Dad.

And yet, I managed to remove all but traces of this poison. I bet you're dying to find out how I did it. Don't worry, we will get to it soon enough.

Nothing Speaks Volumes Like Silent Treatment

The last behaviour I need to talk about is silent treatment, the old cold shoulder.

The need to get even with someone you like, for something they most likely didn't even know they did, is so very common. I think that everyone either has this need to get even, or experiences it being done to them. *"I'll show you! You'll be sorry! Don't expect me to be there when you come a lookin'* !" Blatant withholding of love and acceptance. No soup for you! So many Soup Nazis in the world.

Is there any more clear a message that your love is completely conditional? How else could you shout out that if the other person doesn't toe the line, you're not giving them access to your wonderfulness?

Suppose you have a friend, and things seem to be going good and you have hopes of knowing this person for years. Your birthday is coming up, and you expect your friend will do something nice for you. That's what you would do for him. You already have his birthday collected up and put in your phone's calendar. You've thought of how wonderful you will be on his birthday. That's because you expect the same back. The big day - your big day - arrives, and when you see your friend, there's no mention of your birthday.

You are annoyed and feel slighted, marginalized. *"Why didn't he remember my birthday?"* you ask yourself. And here the train jumps the tracks, heading across a barren desert of bad thoughts.

You notice every day that he still hasn't realized it was your birthday last Tuesday. It's been 3 days. You start withholding texts; your subconscious wants to punish him. Taken to extremes, your friendship cools off as you wait for him to fix the problem. The ball's in his court. He's the one who never remembered your birthday!

Do they really owe you in this way? Hmm...

This kind of treatment really puzzles the one it's being used on. They might not be able to even figure it out. What did they do? Is it them at all? Maybe you're just going through something. Maybe the other person will eventually ask you why you're acting this way. By then, you've blown it all out of proportion. You want them to make you feel special so bad... because you can't feel special without them. Yet another person you can't count on. So when they finally ask (or you explode on them without warning), you slice at them like a ninja cutting fruit. They react like a dog that just got kicked right in the face while it was trying to greet you at the door.

What this leads to is you cutting yourself off from the good the world has for you. Whether or not someone "should" have done something is irrelevant. What's important here is the end result for you, and how it makes you feel and act. So one person didn't gush over your birthday. It's just one day. You are now sacrificing any good experiences and friendship growth you could be having with him while you obsess over something that could have been an honest mistake. Is he going out of his way to ignore your birthday in an effort to make you feel lesser, a loser? Of course not! That's what your subconscious mind is for: to make you feel like a loser.

Just ask yourself leading questions, like "Why doesn't he care enough to at least send me a happy birthday text?" Your mind will whisper the answer; it always tries to answer these kinds of questions. Remember Grima Wormtongue whispering in the King's ear in The Lord of the Rings. It tells you that he isn't a very good friend, and maybe he doesn't like you enough to bother. Maybe you aren't really likeable. This leads to the question, why don't I have any good friends? Why can't I find better friends that make me feel the way I deserve?

More thoughts tumble up from the depths. Thoughts of lack; thoughts of always being unloved - not being good enough. Longing for the kinds of friends everyone else seems to have. And now, you are leaking actions into the universe. You snarl instead of smiling, and forget to hold doors open for people. The whole thing snowballs into an avalanche that comes screaming down the hill and wipes out the town of friendship. If you're lucky a few stragglers will escape the snowy death by running in front of it, to come back and be with you. But it will force most people to hold you at a distance. You've become that desperate, needy person that exudes despair. Depression is only a tiny step farther down this path. I know. I've spent months in this trap.

What's the root emotion that causes this whole spiral? Feeling unloved and unwanted. For years, I complained that I couldn't find any worthwhile friends. There wasn't anyone out there who was like me, who understood me. After all of that whining, I had to come to terms with the facts. I was the problem - or rather - my thinking was the problem. And if that was the case, all I had to do was somehow change my thinking. Somehow, I had to stop treating others like they were the cause of my woes.

Now we've covered all of the garbage programming I had from my childhood and you probably see what I mean when I say I was a hot mess. I had a terrible poverty complex. I witnessed anger, alcoholism and spousal abuse. I was a victim of sexual abuse.

This led me to years of depression, and to enter into my own abusive relationships. I struggled to survive materially; I was constantly in debt and unable to manage my affairs. I used anger as a tool, and I had a hard time admitting any of this was a problem.

We are finally getting down to the crux of the matter. I faced my demons, and they were ugly. Now, what?

Interlude

If you stuck around this long, you might be feeling a little down right now. I didn't mean to depress you with all this negative stuff. Maybe you feel empathy for other people's suffering. Maybe this has reminded you of your own experiences. It isn't pretty. And it almost seems hopeless - all of this bad programming trapped in our heads. But it's far from hopeless. Acknowledging a problem is the first step in solving it. It's my opinion that half the battle is in actually taking a look at our actions with a clear head, and honestly considering whether we are on the right track. We don't want to be like a sleepwalker who might fall off a ledge or walk into the road full of oncoming traffic. We need to be awake and guiding our actions.

Maybe - like me - you were forced to admit that you might be at least part of the problem. The initial experiences, beliefs and programs weren't yours, but you kept them going by default. It's a scary place to be, I know.

Now, you want change, even though that seems unlikely. Nothing you tried in the past made a lasting difference. How in the world could you change something that is so deep in your mind, reaching to the very depths of your soul?

Some people get professional therapy, which will help in many ways. It can take a lot of time and money, and isn't guaranteed to "fix" you, but it's well worth the effort. Please find someone to talk to, and explore these issues with an empathetic ear. So much good can come from the help of a good therapist, especially when you think no-one understands what you're going through.

It's definitely a good idea to talk to someone and share your feelings in general. Of course, this needs to be someone you can trust. If you don't have any friends you can confide in, paid professionals are available everywhere, and come with the training needed to help you.

And of course, there are the techniques I promised you. The methods I used to change my programming are virtually free, and compliment any other efforts you make very well. You will be glad to know there are many things you can do to shift from negative baggage and poor results, to positive thoughts and good outcomes. Now we're getting to the good stuff!

In the next chapter, I'll show you how I turned this all around. I went from mindsets and beliefs that were destroying myself and those around me, to peace, happiness, and caring relationships. It all happened in only a fraction of the time it took me to get to that point, and I used techniques that anyone will be able to use. Read on!

Chapter 7

Forgiveness

Let It Go

There's a story about two Zen monks walking from one village to another. The come across a young lady, who needs to get across a stream without getting muddy. There's no bridge nearby, and she pleads with them to help her. With a shrug, one of the monks picks her up and carries her across, putting her down safe and sound on the other side.

His companion is shocked. They've spoken vows to never touch someone of the female persuasion. He looks at his fellow traveller in disbelief, but the other monk simply continues down the path. He follows the transgressor, upset and unable to enjoy the scenery.

They walk for the rest of the day in silence, until they finally stop for the night at a village. Before they enter, the upset monk accosts his friend and asks him how he could have done such a thing as touch the girl. It goes against his vow, and he doesn't seem affected at all. Shocked, the other monk exclaims, "I put her down hours ago, and you are still carrying her around!"

There's no doubt that we carry baggage. The worst baggage can be anger, resentment, or fear; centered on an individual or group who wronged us. Not only did the event happen, but we relive it over and over. Maybe we plan revenge, or replay things we should have said or done in our minds. Maybe we are afraid. Usually, there's a burning resentment and anger, which uses up a lot of our energy.

While it might be true that they escaped justice and deserve consequences, stewing over it doesn't hurt them at all. It hurts us. We can't take care of ourselves when we are stuck in hate and anger. Yes, maybe they deserve to get their own. It would be their just rewards, etc.

But that's irrelevant to you. What should be most important, is your happiness, your healing. If you were happy and whole, you could just let them be.

It's really hard to get past negative emotions like anger. I spent years with a terrible, burning anger at my parents. They let me down in many ways, but a lot of my anger was for my dad being such an unmotivated loser. He completely wasted years

sitting around doing nothing useful. He didn't make an effort to improve; he never seemed to care what he did to all of us. He emotionally abused my mother, my brother, and me. I was poisoned, it was leaking out of me and hurting my wife and kids.

I regret things that I did in anger over the years. I wish I would have forgiven these offenders in my past sooner, but I didn't know how. I knew how angry I was, how destructive it was, but part of me didn't care. It was satisfying in a twisted way, to feel the way I did.

Since I didn't want to confront my father and make my mother's situation worse, I needed a solution. I needed closure, so I could move on. I found a way to easily get that for myself, without anyone's help.

I make them apologize.

I make them beg for forgiveness.

Now, obviously, it isn't easy to get apologies from those who wronged us. I know you already said to yourself, "Yeah, right! That's never going to happen!"

Maybe they aren't actually sorry. Maybe they refuse to talk to us. Maybe we never want to be in the same room with them for the rest of our lives.

Maybe we still have to live near them and don't want to upset the entire apple cart.

Maybe there are others in the situation that you don't want to hurt in the aftermath of a confrontation, ones you think are innocent. My mother still lives with my father, and it would fill me with guilt to make her life harder.

Maybe they're dead.

There's a solution to all of these situations, one that you can definitely use. I promise you, it will do more good for you than you can imagine right now. Have an open mind. This is for you. You deserve to heal and move on.

Super Effective Forgiveness Formula

Get pen and letter paper, and an envelope. Now, write their apology letter, to yourself. Allow them to address it to you. Write it as they would.

Make it good. Add details and times, and have them express how sorry they are, how they wish they could take it back. Make them beg if it seems right. Create an alternative version of the person that truly is devastated by the remorse they have in their heart. They are really hurting with guilt, and they need your forgiveness to go on. List all of the issues, don't hold any of it back. Make them apologize for everything.

Once you finish the letter, get yourself a refreshing drink and go find a private place where you can read the letter out loud. Imagine the individual is there, and make them squirm as they read it to you. They're desperate. You have to listen! They have no idea what to do if you don't hear their apology.

Once you've read it out loud, just sit and think about it quietly. Are you ready to forgive them? Maybe, not yet. They can wait.

This sums up the trouble in you, allows you to examine it in all its misery. You can't hide from the pain and bury it if you want to be free. It has to be exposed and see the light of truth.

When you're ready, write an answering letter forgiving them. It might be right away, or it might be a few days later. This is on your schedule. They committed the offence, you own the outcomes now. They don't deserve your forgiveness; you choose to give it to them if and when you want.

You're In Control, Not Them

In this way, you take back your power. These things were done to you, and now you own the rights to them. They own nothing; they gave away their say in it.

Once you write the answering letter, again get a refreshing beverage and go somewhere private (I suggest green or herbal tea). Be quiet, and then read the letter out loud. Forgive them and let them go, and take responsibility for any outcomes after this point. You are no longer their victim. You're free.

If you want to go a step farther, burn both letters to show yourself you are done. (If you are burning letters, be sure you do it safely! Don't make matters worse by burning down your apartment.)

This has been so helpful for me. I give myself complete permission to move on and do the best I can. The events still happened; there might still be some residual bad feelings and emotional scar tissue. I might never want to see or talk to the individual, but they lost a lot of their hold on me. I usually ended up crying and messy after I'm done, but with a huge sense of relief.

This ritual freed me from anger with my parents. None of us are the same people anymore, and they never understood how angry I was at them or why, but it doesn't matter. I can have a relationship with them that is based in the present, not on all of the old hurts and pain.

It got rid of a lot of the hate I felt to the cousin who sexually abused me all those years ago. He was never going to apologize, since he passed away from AIDS years ago already. The important results are that my mind can heal and move on. I'm not dwelling on what he did to me, how unfair it was. I'm not stuck as a victim.

I encourage you to try this method. It's worth the effort. Take control of the situation and purge the bad feelings as much as you can. Holding on to these resentments and anger we all have inside, is no good for us, so do what is best for you and let them take care of their own soul.

Shouldn't I Confront Them And Make Them Do This For Real?

You might feel that you need to forgive a transgressor in person. This can also be a really good tool to let go of the past. If you are determined or drawn to this route, here are a few things to consider doing.

Talk to a mental health professional about the issue. This is always a good first step that can be very helpful. They can help you decide if it's a good idea to proceed with an in-person forgiving. They will have your emotional and physical safety in mind, and can help keep you from getting into a damaging situation. It's definitely wise to consider all of the consequences of a confrontation, before going ahead with it.

Write down what you plan to say to this person. Remember that in the heat of the moment, you might get lockjaw and not be able to get the words out. There could be some strong emotions running through you, and you don't need to be stammering and lost. You need a script, so what you want to say doesn't get sidetracked. This will be your one chance to have your say, so again, planning is key.

Bring some backup with you, perhaps a good friend. You need support. Make sure this person is on your side, and wasn't a direct part of the situation you need to discuss. A sibling may not be the right person, for example.

Try to make this happen in a neutral place, like a coffee shop or other public location. Things will stay under control if there are plenty of bystanders available to help. Never go to their home, and never invite them to yours for this.

You need to be able to call it off if things go astray, and you can easily walk out of a public venue. It's a lot harder to walk out of your own space or force others to leave.

Stick to forgiving. Don't do any blaming. You know what happened, and you are now forgiving them. If this person doesn't think they did you any harm, then this meeting shouldn't be taking place. Don't put yourself in a situation to fight with them. This is for healing, not hurting.

Takeaways:

1. **Holding grudges, anger, and hate is unhealthy and unproductive.** The only person who pays the price for your negative feelings is you, and maybe those around you that you care for. Your target is probably off enjoying life while you wreck yours with thoughts of ugliness and revenge. Who is the winner?

2. **It is possible to let go of these feelings and move on.** Even if you don't see it now, it is

not only possible to forgive those who wronged you, it's liberating and empowering.

3. **The whole process can be done without confrontation.** There is no need to have any contact with the perpetrators of various past experiences - unless you decide that it is something you need to do.

4. **Forgiving makes you the winner.** That's the way a survivor can look at it. You are stronger and wiser for the experience.

Chapter 8

Change Your Past

Life is clicking right along; you've started changing the course of the stream one stone at a time. Maybe you've tried having someone ask for forgiveness via letter. Even better, if you found a way to forgive them. (Please, please, try this! Don't just read this book and forget about it. It is so worth it to free yourself of resentment and anger at anyone who hurt you in the past.)

If you've done it, you're feeling optimistic. There's a lot more emotional space without that resentment clouding up the joint. You can breathe just a little bit more freely.

But we can't stop and rest yet. Just like a tiny piece of ice sticking out of the ocean could be a huge ship-breaking iceberg, your programming is lurking in the background. It's like a cougar ready to pounce on a defenceless puppy from a tree branch. Save that puppy!

If you knew there was a huge nest of wasps growing on the eaves above your back step, would you leave them there? What if your kid ran out the back door and slammed it, causing the wasps to swarm and stung him or her bad enough that they ended up in the hospital?

What if your best friend was over, and a wasp flew down and stung her in the eye, and she ended up losing that eye?

That wouldn't happen to most people, because they would call an exterminator or buy a can of wasp poison, or whatever it took to get rid of the vermin before something terrible happened.

The experiences and memories that shape your behaviour can be just like those wasps, full of poison and ready to sting. They can, and do, ruin things for you. They need to go.

"But, how? You can't change memories!" You yell at me in frustration. *"What's wrong with you? This isn't Total Recall; I can't just go in and have a memory overhaul. And there's no time machine to go back and*

change history. I'm stuck with the shitty memories and terrible experiences that were forced on me. I'm a product of my environment and there's nothing I can do!"

I understand your view, really I do. It's only normal to think that's true. We can't literally go back and change things.

What we can do is almost as good, though. In fact, it might be better.

"But, but, my precious memories!" some will be saying at this point.

Years ago, I was talking late at night with a friend about our past being a thing that could hold us back. *"If we could change our memories, and erase the bad feeling in our minds, we wouldn't have all these hang-ups and fears,"* I told him. He was really against this idea. Well, actually, he hated it.

"If all of those things are what makes me who I am, I don't want to get rid of them," He told me. *"Even if they were bad, those memories are making me stronger. And they taught me not to trust everyone. I need to protect myself; if I forgot about all of that I could get taken*

advantage of." He decided right there that my idea of moving on free of hang-ups, was a terrible idea.

This was the end of the conversation. I couldn't argue with the logic. But I just knew that memories and beliefs like the ones hard baked into my brain were holding me back big time. I was a hot mess. I was on the verge of total meltdown, hanging on, but hating myself. It was years before I finally found a way to do what needed to be done, but I never forgot the attitude behind my friend's decision.

I proved him wrong. I'm 100 times happier now than I ever was, since I freed myself from the contents of my memory bank. If you have terrible experiences locked up in there that you need to alleviate, we can get this done.

From what you've read in these pages, you already know that your subconscious mind rules your results. It influences your decisions, and actually decides what slice of reality you can see.

Even your body language is a slave to these unconscious forces. As you go through the world, you're giving off signals that change everyone's behaviour around you. You need to kill those wasps!

Without big change at the bottom, you won't see long lasting change. Surface changes are relatively easy, and easily get overshadowed when things get tough. Changing the most self destructive behaviour, such as picking significant others who abuse you, or rage-quitting every job you get, is going to take a big change.

What if I showed you how to keep all the experience and good parts of a memory, still be able to remember exactly what happened, but dull the bad emotional parts of anything that is back there really bothering you? I have done this, used this exact technique on some disgusting and terrifying memories. It's just like they happened to someone else now, and I've actually placed a better version beside the old one.

This probably sounds crazy to you. If it were possible, everyone would do it. Why haven't you heard of this?

First off, it is work. You can't wave a magic wand and get it done.

Secondly, it isn't mainstream to attempt something like this. There are going to be a lot of naysayers and sceptics. A lot of those people will insist their childhood was perfect, too.

Accessing your memories gives you an opportunity to change them, they get rewritten. It's like getting out your favourite book, and each time you open it, you write a little more in the margins. Maybe you highlight things; maybe you stick a piece of paper in there with some notes on it. The information in this book is different now. You could even tear out some pages, or cross out a few lines with a Sharpie.

There's science to back up the idea of changing memories. Donna Jo Bridge is one of the researchers who brought this information to light.

Featured on CNN in the article Your Memory is Like a Game of Telephone, she shows how you can alter each memory every time you bring it back up. This has some very interesting implications.

You can find more information at
http://www.donnajobridge.com/

If we actually alter each memory, bit by bit, then what we have now is just a poor copy of what really happened. And, maybe we made them worse than they really were by focusing on the bad parts so hard. An example would be remembering a car accident that happened 10 years ago. Bringing the incident back, you would naturally zoom in on the pain and the emotional trauma. You might recall traffic zooming by and the disabling fear you were feeling. Those feelings could get amplified with each go around, turning a traumatic event into a massive show stopper that completely debilitates you every time it resurfaces.

But if that's true, the opposite would also be true. Each time we brought the images back, our mind could go the other way and remove the trauma a bit at a time.

The catch is that you have to let your precious suffering go.

You can't identify as a victim anymore. You have to become a survivor who can adapt and conquer. Yeah, things happened, and now we can move on. We have to embrace the idea that growth is possible, and we can take the good while leaving the bad.

Back to the car accident. Previously you might have focused on the broken glass and the mess left on the pavement by a smashed vehicle. You might have seen flashing emergency vehicle lights; maybe you sustained injuries. Let's leave those for a minute. Was there anything else?

How about helpful bystanders? Kind words from strangers? Was the sun shining? Did loved ones show up to help you? Were you incredibly lucky to have survived, was it a miracle? You could focus on all of these things, instead of the screaming and the injuries.

All we need now is a way to frame the memory slightly differently, and we can change our mind about the whole thing.

This doesn't only apply to bad memories.

There's a whole frontier of positive energy we can gain by amping up our good memories.

Every time we remember that summer camping trip, we can emphasize our favourite parts. Think about drinks around the campfire, walks around the lake, laughing with your friends.

Forget about struggling for an hour trying to light that fire while swatting mosquitoes. Don't worry about how you were woken at five in the morning by those stupid loud crows. If all you bring back is the worst parts, you haven't helped yourself one bit. We are all a cumulative sum of all of our experiences. Why not try to sway your total to the positive instead of the negative numbers?

I know I'm mostly discussing how to remove negative programming. We don't need to leave a vacuum, we can simultaneously eliminate the negative while implanting a positive.

Let's change a memory.

Come on I'll walk you through it. It's really quite easy.

We are going to start with a quick meditation to calm things down upstairs. Just sit still and breathe for a few minutes, nothing fancy. We don't need the equivalent of rocket science here, or brain surgery. **We want rocket surgery!**

Or maybe, just a calm space. Make sure you're sitting upright in a place where you won't be bothered for a little while. I recommend sitting instead of lying down, but only to keep you from falling asleep as easily.

Now, let's pull up a happy memory.

Don't worry, we aren't changing this one!

This could be something like the smiling face of your son or daughter as they play. It could be the day you bought that new car and drove it off the lot. Any memory that brings a smile to your face and you are glad about.

Just enjoy the happy memory for a few seconds. Actually feel any feelings attached in it. Don't rush; try to imagine you are back there for real. Bask in the good feelings.

Everyone will be at a different place with this exercise. Most people are visual learners and find it easy to see mind pictures. These things usually get better with practice, so you might need to give this a few tries to really see what you're trying for. If you don't see any pictures, just focus on the feelings to start with.

For Good Memories, See Them As If They Are Actually Happening To You Again

For memories that you want to amplify, the important thing to do is to imagine them as if you are actually there. You should see through your eyes as if it is happening again. *If you held up your hand in the memory, you should see your hand in front of your eyes* . You shouldn't be able to see your face. You aren't watching this happy memory on a screen, you're living it.

And even more important to understand, is that when you bring up a sad memory, you want to watch it on a screen away from your body. You want to see yourself on that screen, away from yourself. When you watch a mind movie of the event and see yourself in it enacting the memory, you create distance. *Distancing yourself from the bad memory means it loses impact and recedes in importance* . If you put yourself directly in your body in the memory, your mind thinks it's happening again for real. The subconscious mind is very literal, and will assume the worst. Your stomach might twist up and your throat may become dry. If you're like me, you might have tears in your eyes when you recall a memory in this way.

We will be looking at a bad recollection in this new way, and that will help remove a lot of the negative energy. Let's give it a try; it will make complete sense to you after a trial run.

Sad Memory Trial Run

Ok. Now, find a sad memory. Don't start with the worst thing you can think of. Pick one to start with that won't be too big of a challenge. For instance, that time you were embarrassed in the checkout line-up at Wal-Mart because you accidentally did something in front of strangers that made you feel foolish. This is a disposable event, because it wouldn't carry as much weight and is safer to practice with, even though it would make a person feel bad.

Take the memory, and put it on a screen in your mind. Move the screen away from you, so you're watching this memory play out from across a room. Go through the event. See those people out there, as though it was a rom-com or a bad drama movie. Then rewind it, and go through it again. Make sure you are totally outside it, watching yourself from afar as though it happened to someone else; because it did happen to someone else. You aren't that person, even if we're talking about a line-up in Wal-Mart, five days ago. You're here, now, and they are back there.

After you watch it a few times, speed it up or slow it down. Change everyone else' clothing, give everyone else in the movie ridiculous props. If a specific person insulted you or made you feel bad, put a rubber unicorn head mask on them and give them a wedgie. Now look at yourself and see your embarrassment, pain, or suffering.

Talk to yourself; let yourself know that you're here for you. If you want, hug them or hold your hand. See how this affects you to know that you're there supporting yourself. Be your friend. Lead yourself out of the memory and take them shopping, or go for ice-cream. See yourself laughing and having a great time. Maybe you end up at the beach with yourself, playing volleyball or swimming.

How did that feel? Are you smiling now at the ridiculousness of this new memory we just fabricated?

Some people will be outraged and worried right now. None of that happened! How can this be healthy?

My argument would be this. You can still tell the difference between this new, happy vision and the original, embarrassing version. The old memory is still there for reference purposes. If you need to actually visit this event, you can. But when you do, you will also remember that the wrongdoer ended up with a unicorn head and a wedgie. You win.

How can it be good for you to feel embarrassed and crappy every time you go to Wal-Mart and remember this stupid throwaway event? It's so much healthier for you to smile when you think about your adversary wearing a unicorn head in the checkout line like some sort of freak.

This will take the edge right off of a sad memory.

It doesn't erase it. Any important life lessons are still there. The big difference is that it no longer has as much of an impact on you anymore.

I've used this on my worst memories; I've been there for myself when I was a confused boy being forced to perform sex acts at the age of five. **I rescued myself, because no one else would.** I made sure that little boy knew he was safe, loved and protected. I took him right out of that hard spot and changed his life.

I can now examine any part of that memory without any sad feeling whatsoever. I know it still happened, there's no changing the facts. Except now, the outcome for my soul is entirely different.

I can look at a new version of those events. I see myself playing in a massive playground with other children on the day that this would have happened. There's a big sandbox, and I have all of my Tonka Trucks and army men in full battle array. We have a great time until the sun goes down and my parents take me home.

None of that happened. I didn't have fancy toys like that, and we didn't go to any such playground. I wasn't friends with any other boys. None of that matters because it feels like I did, and the really bad things are nullified.

Do you have any traumas that are holding you back? If you've had enough and desperately need a way out of bad experiences from your past, you need to give this a try. It will work wonders, and it costs you nothing except a little bit of quiet time.

Imagine how the course of your life might have gone if a few terrible things didn't ever happen. Have you always been shy because a bully always made fun of you every time you tried to talk to the other children? What if you removed that bully and saw yourself laughing and playing with the other kids? If that became real, it might transform your now self.

Imagine your mind as a set of sliding switches, like a graphic equalizer for music. These switches can be moved one at a time, and each switch on either side of the one being moved will slide just a bit as well. So, moving the first switch a bit in an upward, positive direction will move all of the other switches since they're all tied together.

Changing a memory in this way sends ripples forward through the whole brain.

It's like time travel without the science fiction part. Without that bully, your whole life jumps to a new track. Instead of a loser on the sidelines, you become slightly more popular. This ends up with you getting that date for the prom that you wanted, and you have more friends. You're a bit happier all the way through.

The ripple travels all the way through time right to now. Looking back, you're a bit happier with yourself. You love yourself that much more, and you're a bit more successful. It's a win-win scenario. There's nothing to lose. You get to have your cake, and eat it too.

Now, you have one powerful tool to eradicate that wasp nest on the back porch of your mind. You can find those pockets of darkness and shine light on them, taking away their power. You can go into the back yard of your mind and safely enter your garden. You're ready for the next step, planting seeds and growing yourself a crop of beautiful flowers and fruit trees. Next, I will show you how you can plant those seeds to grow the kind of thoughts that will benefit you the most. Your mind will produce amazing and fruitful thoughts that will take you places you can only dream of.

Takeaways:

1. **Negative, traumatic memories can sabotage your happiness.** They lie in wait, like a snake in the grass, for something to trigger them. They need to be dealt with.

2. **Memories aren't solid, unchanging, and immovable.** Researchers have shown that every time we bring a memory out, it is altered slightly. We can't be certain that we even remember the true events.

3. **We can choose to alter our memories.** If we decide to, we can amplify, dilute, or even replace memories. In fact, we already do this, all we need to do is learn to direct it.

Chapter 9

The Power of the Question

In the last chapter, we found out how good memories can be amplified, and how you can destroy the power bad memories have on you. Next, we need tools to help us change thought patterns that aren't helping us, replacing them with thoughts which encourage growth and happiness.

The majority of our thought processes are subconscious, below the surface. Since we can't see what's going on down there, it's easy to come to the conclusion that we have little control over these thoughts. This isn't necessarily true. When leading a large animal like a horse to water, you can either try to force it to follow you, or you can nudge it and encourage it to do what you want. That's what we will do here. I can show you one tool you can use to nudge your subconscious mind and get the results you want much easier than trying to force it.

Imagine there are two paths in front of you, which start out going in roughly the same direction. They diverge fairly soon, one of them leading to a beautiful meadow and then on to a large park with a big fountain in the centre. The other path starts out a little rocky, then goes through a ravine, and on into a dank, old, rotting forest with a still pool at the centre. This pool has a scum of algae growing on it. Totally an amazing picnic spot (if you're Gargamel from The Smurfs).

You have a beautiful and friendly horse named Sarge, but he has a bit of a knack for strong headedness. He has a mind of his own and will trample you if you don't stay on his good side. You want to lead your horse to water, it's a hot day and he's thirsty. As you take the lead rope in your hands, you ask yourself, *"How can I get old Sarge here the drink he needs?"* You notice that when you speak kindly and positively to Sarge, he moves to the nicer path and heads toward the meadow. But if Sarge gets it in his mind to go toward the less appetizing path, he pulls you along with him. Now you're the passenger instead of the guide!

Treating your subconscious mind the wrong way will end up with a trip to the scum pond.

No one enjoys a drink from this pond, with water you almost need to chew.

We want to end up at the nice fountain with clear water, obviously. And we can get there. But we need our subconscious mind working with us, not against us. And this is surprisingly easy to accomplish. All we need to do is ask ourselves the right questions, give our subconscious the right nudges.

Let's examine the power of the question.

Posing the right question is amazingly effective to get both positive and negative results. Questions to yourself activate the most powerful computer you have access to - the subconscious mind. It has a huge store of information, and not only that, it can start looking for new patterns and information to help or hinder you. Start with the right queries in the morning to get this computer on a solving mission. Ask the wrong questions and it will work all day to get the negative answers you requested. In fact, this might be one thing that is constantly holding you back all this time. Unknowingly, you could be asking yourself leading questions that cause a cascade effect through your brain and give you results you don't want.

You just don't want the world's most powerful computer trying to explain why something is bad. It will lay it out for you in detail. I watched this play out in my family all the time. My father would, out loud, ask himself the most terrible questions. This was a huge clue to me; it laid the foundation for my eventual escape from my personal black iron prison. Here's an example of his thought train, which he generously provided for us by his speaking out loud in front of his children, in an exaggerated show of self pity.

"Why can't I finish our new house? Oh well, I'll never get it finished now," He said one night and shook his head. Then he started answering his own question out loud. The weather was terrible; the farm wasn't doing very good. The economy was bad. Those people down the road cheated him out of money that we needed for building supplies. These answers had him thinking about even more bad things. Politics came into it of course. He led his horse right into the dank old forest and gave it water out of a stagnant pond. Then it was time to take it out on the whole family, yelling at us how stupid we were.

What if he had known what was happening? Could he have somehow changed the direction of his thoughts? I think it's totally possible to change the way you look at things. All it takes is the initial urge to do better, saying yes to the world just once.

Let's examine a few sample negative questions, and then move on to their positive counterparts. What if you were unfortunate enough to ask yourself this: *"Why don't I have more friends?"* Your mind is going to answer you if this question gets formulated, without fail. It will come up with lots of useful gems that make you feel really bad about yourself. You aren't very likeable. You're not very attractive.

Your personality gets in the way. You suck. Sarge pulls at the rope and you head down that rocky path of self hate.

We need to be aware that reframing our questions can help. Don't worry right now how we will pull this off - I will show you that later. For now, just wrap your brain around the premise that we always ask ourselves these questions, and they are the keys to the kingdom of our subconscious.

What is the positive thought to counteract this one? It would be *"How can I make some amazing new friends?"* Several answers pop up out of your subconscious mind. You could join some sort of club, take dancing lessons, or maybe join a beer league sports team. You could take your dog to the dog park. You could check for local groups online that have similar interests. There are so many ways that you could find more friends, and you might have come up with more just by reading this. You've just convinced your horse Sarge into walking through that meadow.

Next scenario: You are at home anxiously waiting for your teenage daughter to get home. She recently started driving her own car, and any parent has heightened fears at times like these. She's 20 minutes late for curfew.

Your brain goes into overdrive, prompted by questions like this one. *"Why isn't my daughter home yet? What if something happened to her?"* Here we go: a train wreck of terrible thoughts that will bury you in fears and doubts. You consider every conceivable (negative!) thing that could have happened to your daughter to stop her from arriving on time. Car accidents, muggings, rape, you name it.

It's all your fault, because you let her drive. She isn't ready. Now you destroyed her life. And yours, with this totally unproductive thinking. But this helps you be ready, some people think. I don't know about you, but I can live just fine without being ready to suffer. I'm all for being ready to prosper and be happy! Change your questions, change your life!

What questions could counteract this one? It's definitely a tough one. How about this? *"What kind of legitimate and safe things could be causing her to be late and not call me?"* Now we get some answers like this: her phone might have gone dead, and she lost track of time. She decided to chat with a friend, and forgot to text you to let you know. She is stuck in traffic and is ignoring her phone because she's driving – after all, you taught her well.

When she pulls in 10 minutes later, you see that everything will be okay. Any worrying you might have done accomplished nothing except creating a lot of tension in you.

Ask the wrong questions after a hard work day, and before you know it, your mind is buzzing with anxiety and worry. *"I wonder what's going to happen tomorrow with that mix-up over the presentation. I hope that John won't be mad about that email I sent. I wonder if this is going to spiral out of control."* This is a clear invitation to your own personal mega-computer to find some answers of how bad things could get. John might turn everyone at the office against you. What if he sabotages the project and you end up getting fired?

To reframe this, you would have to counter with something like *"How can I show John that I respect him and want him on my side?"* Then you might think of things like, *"I can take him a Starbucks tomorrow morning and let him know I appreciate his contributions on last month's invoices."*

I hope you can see the difference. One way of thinking leaves you wide open for any sort of direction. The other nudges your brain into having actual positive and helpful thoughts. Thoughts create emotional states. We want to guide our emotional states so we end up at the fountain in the park, not at the dank forest with the scum covered pond. In the next chapter I will show you easy ways to use this in your favour every day. This has changed my life immeasurably, and I know it will help you too.

Takeaways:

1. **Life is either yes or no.** We chose, moment by moment, to say yes to life, or no.

2. **One thing leads to another.** Just like the eighties song by The Fixx, negatives start stacking up and leading to more negatives.

3. **We can choose to stack up positives instead!** Seeding the right thoughts will lead to good things in our lives, happier thoughts, and better feelings.

Demons in the Cellar

Chapter 10
Questioning Reality

Dogs can be programmed with treats and cuddles, and bells.

Jason Bourne was reprogrammed with drugs and sleep deprivation, as well as psychological manipulation.

Now it's your turn to be reprogrammed.

Sadly, after we're done, you won't be an international spy.

You'll be the next best thing, though. You'll be a super sleeper agent. You'll look just like everyone else, but you'll be more effective and happier.

We aren't going to use any sleep deprivation, mind altering drugs, or even bells and treats to reprogram your subconscious mind. It just doesn't require that much work. In fact, it's so downright simple, anyone can do it.

All this is going to take is a little thought, a pen and paper, and a small amount of determination. It seems to help to use concrete, physical actions of writing down the questions, rather than typing them, but typing the words might work well for some of you.

I want you to write down a question to yourself, one that presupposes good things about you or the near future.

For example: *How can I have an amazing day?* As soon as you write this question, off your subconscious mind goes to find a way to make this happen. You can call a friend at lunch break. You can plan your big trip next fall and get the house cleaned up. You can line up a movie with friends after work. There's no end of ways for your subconscious mind to make this an amazing day.

I can sense your doubt, but this really works. Posing that leading question to yourself in writing will transform the way you think.

How about this one: *What can I do to make someone else really happy today?*

This is a powerful one. How about pick up some flowers and stop by your mom's house? Send a just because card in the mail? Drop by someone's office and sincerely thank them for their help? Call an employee in and thank them for their hard work and honesty?

You might be getting the picture. It really is that simple.

Another thing I've been asked, isn't this just an affirmation? No, it isn't. An affirmation is a statement that you have decided to repeat to yourself in an attempt to trick your subconscious mind into believing it's true. *"Every day, in every way, I'm healthier, wealthier, and happier ."* This probably works for some people. It never worked for me, and I think that's because my brain knew it was a lie. I spent a lot of time experimenting with the affirmation type of positive thinking, years in fact. I had poor results.

When I switched to framing myself a question, I got results in days. Days!

Back to your seed question. You want to get some positive motion in the old brain, and avoid things which might seem positive but could actually be negative. *"Why"* can be bad. *"Why is this business not working?"* This one can give you answers like, *"Because no one likes our products"* or *"because we aren't good enough,* or *"because nothing I do ever works out and I'm a failure."* This is exactly what happens inside 99.9% of the world's population, they undermine themselves.

You want to support and love yourself instead. "What can I do today to help my business succeed?" This might pop out the ideas, "I could brainstorm some new product ideas," "Maybe I will contact some existing customers and ask for testimonials," or "It's time to do some advertising!"

Other business and carrier related questions could be "How could I earn an extra 1000 this month?", or "What's the best direction for my career?"

The goal here is to switch the focus and let you see some new things. You were looking in the rear view mirror, using the lens of programming to filter everything. By changing the viewpoint just slightly, you're now looking forward and seeing some opportunities.

Here's some seed questions that can get a person's mind looking for gold: How can I do great at my job and get ahead in life?

What is it about me that people love?

When is the best time to surprise them with my presence?

How many times can I get someone to smile today?

What is the sexiest thing about my wife/husband?

Questions that won't help you out contain the words no, not, don't, why, can't, and won't. Avoid these ones:

Why can't I find more friends?

Why does everything I do go to heck? How come I don't have someone to love?

These are obviously all terrible and of no help.

Ok, it's your turn. Got your pen? Write a couple questions down that really feel good to you. I'm going with this one: "How can I make someone's day?"

Go ahead and write! (On paper, please, not on the screen!)

_____

_____

Don't be fooled by the simplicity of this idea.

Everything has a beginning. The biggest business on earth started out as a small idea that someone took and focused on to grow it. On the other hand, any murder that involves planning also started out as a single idea that was carefully nurtured.

All we are doing here is planting a seed, watering it, and then waiting for it to grow. Soon enough, a vine will spring up and take a life of its own. Then, it's only a matter of time before you have melons, baby!

We aren't limited to questions by any means. As long as it's a statement that gently guides your thoughts in the right direction, instead of trying to force belief.

Try the feel of this one: *"I'm thinking how great it would be to make some new friends this week."* This one just seems like wishful thinking, doesn't it? How can this affect the real world? Easy!

Now, your subconscious mind is looking for the friends it knows out there. That part of your mind isn't super bright. It only knows what it gets for input. Now it's looking for these great friends you mentioned. Where are they? This outward focus changes your perceptions, and you react just a bit different. Maybe you get outside yourself and find yourself talking to people you normally wouldn't, and end up making plans to meet someone this weekend. It might not be your new best friend, but it's a connection you wouldn't have made before.

The ones I use the most are "wouldn't it be easy" and "wouldn't it be nice". I get amazing results with them, almost like magic! *"Wouldn't it be nice if I could get to be good friends with _____ "* has helped me approach people I never would have talked to, for example.

Let's move on, so I can show you how to take the idea of a seed thought and turn it into a powerful ritual that will have amazing results!

Hopefully, in the previous chapter, you came up with at least one question that called out to you. For demonstration purposes, I'm going to use one to increase happiness about work and day to day life.

"How can I have fun and get ahead today?"

Alright, we have your first mind seed all ready, now how do we plant it?

I suggest first thing in the morning. My phone is an important part of this process. I set my regular alarm, get up, and go about things. Ten minutes after I'm awake and a little less fuzzy, I have an alert set that puts the question on my screen. In this day and age, almost everyone is already using a screen of some sort first thing in the day; you could use a tablet screen, or you could even set your question as your computer background.

Then, as soon as I can, I get to my journal and write it out. I say it out loud a couple to times to lock it in. I just sit quietly and brainstorm for a few seconds to get the ideas going. And that's it. Crazy easy. I'm ready to head out the door, and I feel like I've already accomplished something big. I start my day out with accomplishment instead of the morning blahs.

First thing in the morning sets the tone for the day.

It primes you for action. Starting your day with a morning routine is pivotal in creating happy, successful days, and I believe that starting early sets the right tone. This mind seed fits right in with that philosophy.

Think about it this way: Getting this thought in there early in the day is like making sure you're aimed down the driveway before you put the car in drive. If you start out in a straight line, you're less likely to run over a bike on the lawn and take out the mailbox. Just leaping out of bed and sprinting to work, leaves you prey to whatever seed that you run into. You could end up basing your day on a billboard sign, or something your spouse said while you were getting ready for work, or some other random input from the world. Your mind can be a finely tuned instrument, but garbage in, equals garbage out. To get the results you want, you need to fill the gas tank with premium fuel.

As your day progresses, you could follow this up with another alert on your phone, or on your computer. Maybe timed for coffee time or lunch, your alert could pop up to remind you. I do this frequently. It's a good way to remind yourself of your intentions to seed thoughts.

Do you have a bedtime routine? This is another huge opportunity to get your subconscious working for you. Add a question to your routine. If you write out your mind seed before bed, your subconscious will work on it while you sleep. This is a rarely used technique that masters such as Neville used in their teachings.

Before bed, you might be more calm and receptive. Following the same procedure, write your question out with a pen and paper. Then say it out loud or in your head a couple times. Good night.

This Is The Magic Ingredient Behind A Gratitude Journal

Many people keep a gratitude journal, as a way to bring more abundance into their lives. There are entire books written about this practice. At it's most basic level, this journal is presupposing something positive about your day. When you go to write in your gratitude journal, you are asking yourself, *"what am I grateful for, what good things happened to me?"*

That's all the invitation your personal mega-computer needs to go digging. Turns out it found a few things. You're grateful for a hug from your daughter, maybe. Grateful for clean water and a warm house. Grateful to live in North America instead of a war torn country.

As soon as you practice gratitude, you utilize the power of the question to improve your mindset. It works even better if you know what's going on!

If the best way for you personally to use the power of questions is a gratitude journal, then I encourage you to start one today. Write in it every morning, or every evening. It will make a world of difference.

"It seems too simple. Can you make it a little more complicated so I can believe it's real?"

Sure!

Now that we have some good seed thoughts and questions swirling around in our brains, starting to change things slowly but surely, can we boost the effects of these positive influences? You bet.

A super simple meditation can help more than most people imagine. It doesn't have to involve sitting silently with your legs all twisted up for hours a day, unless you want it to. Just a few minutes a day is enough to start.

It's best to begin practicing this in a quiet location where you won't be disturbed. This will help you focus, and keep you from feeling self conscious if other people are around. If you are doing this first thing in the morning, it's easier to arrange a quiet spot than later on in the day.

Here's the super simple meditation anyone can pull off:

1. **Stop moving. Sitting upright with a straight back, is the best.**

2. **Set a timer. Start with 5 minutes and increase over time.**

3. **Breathe. It doesn't matter how you breathe to start, just let yourself breath in and out, and notice it happening. Feel the effects as**

the oxygen travels to your lungs and your blood courses through your limbs.

4. Watch things. Watch things go by your mental window as you would sitting in the window seat of a bus. Watch the wall. Watch any boring thing until you see how not boring it is...

5. Let it be easy. If you start becoming sidetracked thinking about work or X- men movies or Shades of Grey, or whatever, as soon as you notice - just watch a breath go by.

That doesn't sound too hard, does it? We are only talking five minutes here, people.

Maybe you've tried it before and it didn't work out for you. Give it another shot; it takes repetition to really get it rolling.

What is this meditation going to do for you? A lot more than you would expect from such a simple activity! It actually changes the structures of the brain slowly but surely. It gives you more space to think by slowing things down, which is like cleaning of the mental table so you have some room to get down to business. There are hundreds of books and articles on how great meditation can be. I urge you to check them out.

Also, adding this to daily ritual can have a cumulative effect on your willpower and personal accountability. You feel more in control. It's your thing. You can slowly increase meditation time as you wish, or keep it at five minutes every day.

Now that you've calmed your mind, this is a perfect time to use your seed question or statement.

You'll be more receptive to the suggestions of your mind, and it will supercharge the rest of the day for you.

Mental work is a good way to get to know the real you. We spend some time with people at work, a lot of time with family and friends, maybe a good percentage of our day might be with our small children. *The biggest percentage of our time is spent with ourselves.* One hundred percent of our time is in fact spent with ourselves. So don't we owe it to ourselves to get to know us a little better? Most of us are in constant motion, running from one activity to another like crazed teenagers at a mall. Slowing down, sitting and observing ourselves, maybe going for a coffee with ourselves afterward, this will lead to liking ourselves a little more.

Takeaways:

1. **You can easily program yourself for positive thoughts and better outcomes.**

   You just have to ask the right questions, and your behaviours will change.

2. **Avoid asking yourself why. Leading questions with the word why begets negative and depressing answers.** Once your subconscious mind gets permission to tell you all the sad reasons why, it will unleash a

barrage of unhelpful and unhealthy thoughts of doom and despair.

3. **Start your day off with a leading seed question that pre-supposes you are a talented winner.** You could literally ask yourself, *"What can I do today to prove how much of a talented winner I am?"* Your subconscious mind will scramble to show you what you can do. And you will indeed be a talented winner soon enough.

4. **Meditation before the seed question will amplify your results.** Calming your mind with meditation is like working the soil before planting.

Chapter 11
The Dramatic Conclusion

There are many paths through life. Many think that the best path would be an eternal happy dance, with no cares or worries. It sounds fantastic!

This path would be flat and smooth, so you couldn't trip. No little hills or valleys; only flat trails with plenty of flowers on the edges. And don't forget the obedient servants to dispense drinks. With little umbrellas!

There should be places to sit and rest. Actually, why bother walking down the path any farther? Everything is the same everywhere, might as well just sit down and be waited on by the friendly and obliging servers. Maybe if we had some video games, hot wings, and beer?

And thus would end all progress for many people, or at least slow it down. This is similar to the future blob humans of the movie Wall-E, everyone relaxing and swilling high energy liquid refreshments as they get fatter and less mobile, all the while ignoring reality to be distracted by electronics.

Then there is a more realistic path. We encounter good and bad. There are long, boring stretches with no flowers or refreshments. Sometimes a crevasse blocks our way. We might trudge up hills, through blizzards, and then through sunshine. Fruit trees might supply us with amazing wild bounty. We might go hungry for a while.

And eventually, we can climb high above the surrounding plains. We can take the paths less followed, up steep and rocky trails to the summits of human experience. We can wend our way around the edges of cliffs, between huge boulders, past pure mountain lakes with still, cold, blue water.

From here, we can see out over the path we followed for so long. We can look down on the prairie and the forest, and remember the various trials we encountered. And we can also see the good moments, the amazing experiences we lived through. We can get perspective on things that we never could before.

If you are one of the lucky souls who reaches the summit, you will see that everything you went through was necessary to get you to this moment.

I know that anyone reading these words will have lived through amazing times. Congratulations! I hope you can see how special you are, how amazing this human experience really is.

My own personal journey has been very challenging. But I never gave up, I plodded through until I found the foothills, then I started trying to climb those mountains. Eventually, I found a way to start gaining some altitude, after several false starts up dead end trails and having to backtrack.

I haven't quite made it to that peak yet. But even from the vantage point half way to the top, I can turn and look down, and I see others struggling through swamps and clouds of mosquitoes down below.

I want to help in any way I can, to make sure everyone keeps on the path. It's a terrible thing, to know that there are people out there who quit because they feel alone and can't find a way to go on. Writing these words is one of the ways I hope to reach out to someone in need.

Hopefully, sharing my story will help give someone courage or hope, or at least let them know they aren't alone.

There were times when I was at my lowest points, where I desperately needed help. It was rare that anyone reached out. Everyone is absorbed in their own stories; too busy worrying about themselves to see that others are struggling so hard.

I try to remember this when I come across that stranger in public who is obviously irate or in a really bad frame of mind. I don't know their path. I don't know what led them here. All I can see is that this person is extremely disgruntled and unfriendly.

All I can try to do is not increase their load. When you see someone barely above water, almost drowning, should you push down on their head and see if you can force them under? No! So then, why would we try to "push someone's buttons" and send them over the edge?

When I have a co-worker that is causing difficulty for me, I try to remember that they are operating out of different beliefs and programming than me. It isn't personal unless I make it personal. I try to be harmless. I know it isn't easy, but who wants to be harmful? There's already enough harm in the world.

After hearing my early childhood story, you might think I hate my parents and never visit them. The opposite is in fact true. I've climbed high enough on the mountain that I can turn around with enough perspective to see the truth.

My parents were the product of their own terrible childhoods. Things were difficult for them. They were exposed to rigid beliefs and thinking from all sides. They lived though poverty and lack. Society was very constrictive.

They were abused, bullied, and pushed around. They had their own demons in the cellar.

It might be that they did the best they could; they did what their programming told them too. So, I forgive them. And in any case, they gave me the environment I must have needed to get to this point.

The tables are turned. I am now a caregiver, and they need my help. And I will gladly give it to them.

We are all connected, and everyone is valuable. Be good to each other. Lend a helping hand on the trail. I hope to see you at the summit one day!

Dedication

A big thanks to my wife, Nicole, for sticking with me through the tough times. Thanks to Bethany, Eric and Andrew for turning out to be amazing human beings. Thanks to the universe for providing me with the basic building blocks of success, like carbon, DNA and coffee. Thanks to Self Publishing School and launch team members for inspiration, accountability and assistance.

I appreciate the time you spent with me. Thank you for reading!

If this book spoke to your heart, pass it on to someone else who could use it. Refer it to a friend.

If you have an Amazon account, please take a moment and write a few words - leave a helpful and honest review on Amazon.com. It would help a ton!

Here's the link:

https://www.amazon.com/Demons-Cellar-Reprogram-Subconscious-Shackles-ebook/dp/B01M64OXQA

Let others know what you thought - it would mean a lot to me. Every review or referral is just one more reason that that someone in need can use to justify reading this book. Help me reach more people, and together we can change the world!

Thank you!

Made in United States
North Haven, CT
17 May 2022

19225103R00096